Volume

BLACKBIRCH PRESS

An imprint of Thomson Gale, a part of The Thomson Corporation

THOMSON

GALE

Detroit • New York • San Francisco • San Diego • New Haven, Conn. • Waterville, Maine • London • Munich

Consultant: Kimi Hosoume
Associate Director of GEMS (Great
  Explorations in Math and Science),
Director of PEACHES (Primary
  Explorations for Adults, Children,
  and Educators in Science),
Lawrence Hall of Science,
University of California,
Berkeley, California

For The Brown Reference Group plc
Text: Chris Woodford
Project Editor: Lesley Campbell-Wright
Designer: Lynne Ross
Picture Researcher: Susy Forbes
Illustrator: Darren Awuah
Managing Editor: Bridget Giles
Children's Publisher: Anne O'Daly
Production Director: Alastair Gourlay
Editorial Director: Lindsey Lowe

PHOTOGRAPHIC CREDITS
The Brown Reference Group plc: Edward Allwright 1, 12, 13t, 14, 28–29, Susy Forbes 9t;
Corbis: Paul Barton 15, Terry W. Eggers 24, ESA/PLI 21, Najlah Feanny 11b, Firefly
Productions 25, Gunter Marx Photography 7, Don Mason 10, Roger Ressmeyer 23,
Reuters 19; **NASA:** 4–5, 5b, 27t; **Photos.com:** 5t, 9b, 11t, 13, 17, 22, 26.

Front cover: **The Brown Reference Group plc:** Edward Allwright

LIBRARY OF CONGRESS CATALOGING-IN-PUBLICATION DATA

Woodford, Chris.
  Volume / by Chris Woodford.
    p. cm. — (How do we measure?)
  Includes bibliographical references.
  ISBN 1-4103-0367-5 (lib. bdg. : alk. paper) — ISBN 1-4103-0523-6 (pbk. :
alk. paper)
  1. Volume (Cubic content)—Juvenile literature. 2. Area measurement—Juvenile
literature. I. Title II. Series: Woodford, Chris. How do we measure?

QA465.W68 2005
530.8—dc22
                        2004019138

Printed and bound in Thailand
10 9 8 7 6 5 4 3 2 1

Contents

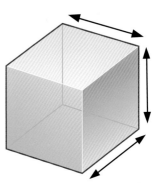

What is volume?

One of the world's biggest airplanes is called the Airbus Beluga. It is named for a whale called the beluga. This airplane is so huge that it has enough space inside to carry about 50,000 basketballs. Another large airplane, the Boeing 747 Jumbo Jet, can carry almost 30,000 basketballs. A station wagon is much smaller. It can probably carry only 50 to 100 basketballs.

The amount of space something can hold is called its volume. An Airbus Beluga

This gigantic airplane is an Airbus Beluga. It is one of the world's biggest airplanes. It has a huge volume, so it can carry lots of things.

has more volume than a Jumbo Jet because it can hold more things. A station wagon has less volume than a Jumbo Jet because it can hold fewer things.

Volume and space

We can also think of volume another way. Volume is the amount of space something takes up. Fifty thousand basketballs take up a certain volume. And that is the same as the volume inside an Airbus Beluga airplane.

Measuring by comparing

We can measure a large volume by finding out how many times a smaller volume fits inside it. We do this when we say that an airplane holds 50,000 basketballs. We are measuring the airplane's volume by comparing it with the volume of a basketball.

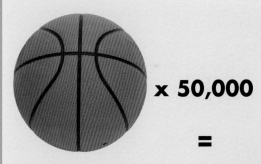

x 50,000

=

Length, area, and volume

A longer airplane usually has more volume than a shorter one. Length is not the only thing that changes volume, though. Suppose we could make the airplane wider or higher but keep it the same length. That also increases the airplane's volume.

Just as volume is linked to length, it is also linked to area. Area is the size of a flat surface.

Three dimensions

Length is a measurement in one direction. Sometimes we call this direction a dimension. To measure an area, we usually have to measure both its length and width. So area is a measurement in two directions, or dimensions. To find something's volume, we have to measure it in three directions. So, volume is a measurement in three dimensions: length, height, and width.

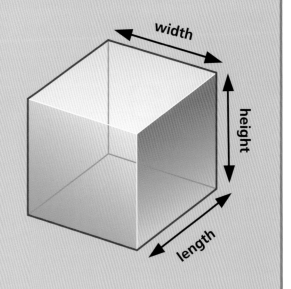

length x height x width = volume

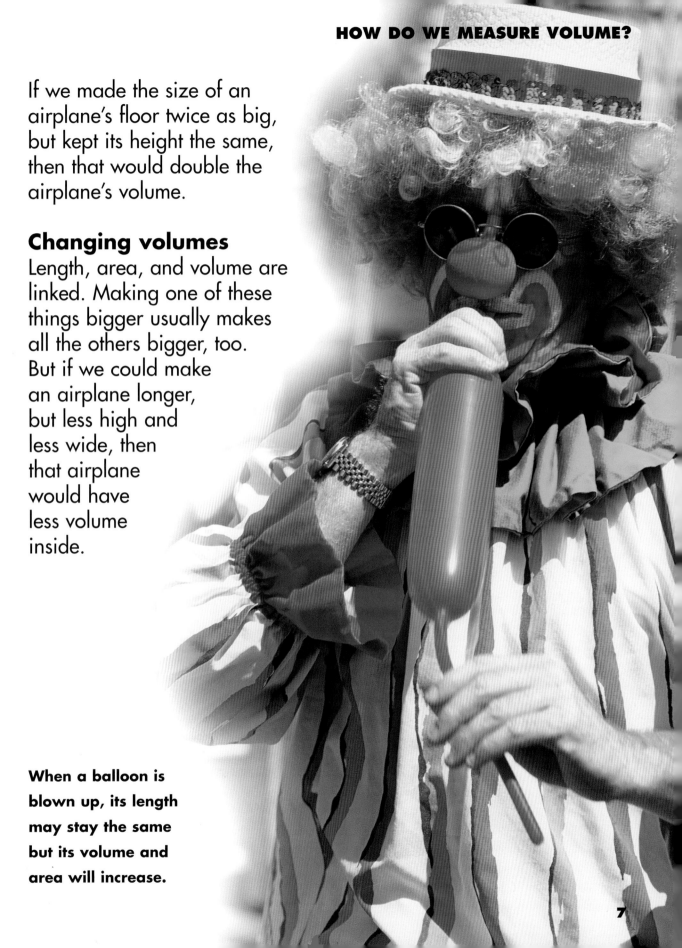

If we made the size of an airplane's floor twice as big, but kept its height the same, then that would double the airplane's volume.

Changing volumes

Length, area, and volume are linked. Making one of these things bigger usually makes all the others bigger, too. But if we could make an airplane longer, but less high and less wide, then that airplane would have less volume inside.

When a balloon is blown up, its length may stay the same but its volume and area will increase.

Cubic units

We can measure large volumes by seeing how many basketballs we can fit inside them. But what if we want to be more accurate than that? We could start by measuring the volume of just one basketball. A basketball is a sphere. Very roughly, it measures 1 foot long, by 1 foot wide, by 1 foot high.

So its volume is about the same as a cube that measures 1 foot by 1 foot by 1 foot. Another way to say this is that the volume of a basketball is 1 cubic foot. A cubic foot is a volume that measures 1 foot in each direction.

Each unit of length has a matching unit of volume. We can measure small volumes

---

You can estimate the volume of a sphere such as a basketball by fitting it inside an imaginary cube. An estimate is a good guess.

To make your estimate close to the real figure, the cube must be a tight fit. The cube around this basketball is 1 foot long, tall, and wide.

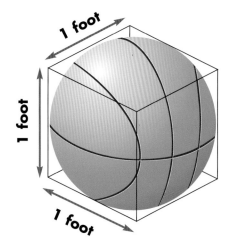

1 foot

1 foot

1 foot

length x height x width = volume

1 foot x 1 foot x 1 foot = 1 cubic foot

(1 x 1 x 1 = 1)

This is 1 cubic inch.

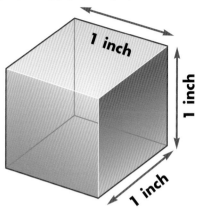

1 cubic foot = 12 inches x
12 inches x 12 inches
= 1,728 cubic inches

1 cubic yard, or 27 cubic feet
= 36 inches x 36 inches x 36
inches = 46,656 cubic inches

1 cubic mile = 1,760 yards
x 1,760 yards x 1,760 yards
= 5½ billion cubic yards

in cubic inches. A cubic inch
measures 1 inch long, by
1 inch wide, by 1 inch high.
We can measure larger volumes
in cubic yards or even cubic
miles. A cubic mile measures
1 mile long, by 1 mile
high, by 1 mile wide.

Typical volumes

Volume of a regular dictionary
= 30 cubic inches

Volume inside a station wagon
= 150 cubic feet

Volume of a swimming pool
= 132,000 cubic feet

Volume of a Boeing 747 Jumbo
Jet = 30,000 cubic feet

Liquid volumes

People need to measure volume when they buy a liquid, such as gasoline. When they fill up their car's gas tank, they buy a certain number of gallons of gas.

1 gallon = 4 quarts = 8 pints
1 quart = 2 pints
1 pint = 16 fluid ounces

A gallon is a measurement of a liquid's volume. It comes from an old word *galleta*, which meant "bucket." In olden times, when you bought a gallon of something, you were really buying a bucketful. A gallon is about the same volume as 230 cubic inches.

These children are making cakes. They are using a measuring cup to add a few fluid ounces of milk to the cake mixture.

The ten-gallon hat

Texans are known for their large ten-gallon hats. But if you filled a ten-gallon hat with water, it would hold only a few pints, not 10 gallons. Ten-gallon hats get their name from *galón*, the Spanish word for "braid," or ribbon. Ten-gallon hats were expensive hats decorated with ten colored braids or ribbons.

A quart is a smaller volume than a gallon. It takes 4 quarts to make a gallon. There are 2 pints in a quart, so there are 8 pints in a gallon.

When people cook, they use a much smaller unit of volume called a fluid ounce. There are 16 fluid ounces in a pint.

This gas pump measures the volume of gasoline that is pumped into a car's tank.

Metric volumes

Pints, quarts, fluid ounces, and gallons are called imperial measures. They are widely used in the United States. In many other countries, people use a different set of measures, called metric measures. Metric measures are based on a unit of length called the meter. A meter is just over 3 feet long. There are 100 centimeters in a meter and 1,000 meters in a kilometer.

A measuring cup often has both metric (liters and milliliters) and imperial (cups and fluid ounces) units along its scale.

This is 1 cubic inch.

1 inch
1 inch
1 inch

1 cm
1 cm
1 cm

This is 1 cubic centimeter (cm³).

Metric cubic units

Just as there are imperial units such as cubic inches, there are also cubic units in the metric system. Small volumes are measured in cubic millimeters or cubic centimeters. Larger volumes are measured in cubic meters or cubic kilometers.

Converting metric and imperial

Dry measures: imperial to metric
1 cubic inch = 16 cubic centimeters
1 cubic foot = ³⁄₁₀₀ cubic meter
1 cubic yard = ¾ cubic meter
1 cubic mile = 4 cubic kilometers

Liquid measures: imperial to metric
1 fluid ounce = 30 milliliters
1 pint = ½ liter or 500 milliliters
1 quart = 1 liter or 1,000 milliliters
1 gallon = 4 liters

Dry measures: metric to imperial
1 cubic centimeter = ⁶⁄₁₀₀ cubic inch
1 cubic meter = 35 cubic feet
1 cubic meter = 1⅓ cubic yards
1 cubic kilometer = ¼ cubic mile

Liquid measures: metric to imperial
1 milliliter = ³⁄₁₀₀ fluid ounces
1 liter = 34 fluid ounces
1 liter = 2 pints
1 liter = ¼ gallon

Liquid measures

There are common liquid measures in the metric system, too. A liter is about the same size as 2 fluid pints, or about a fourth of a gallon. Drinks and gas can be measured in liters.

There are a thousand milliliters in a liter. A doctor or nurse might measure medicine in milliliters. A teaspoon can hold about 5 milliliters.

This pitcher holds about 2 liters (4 pints) of lemonade. The glass holds half a liter (about a pint).

Simple volumes

How can we find out the volume of a simple object, such as a cube, a box, or a pyramid? Usually we need to measure the object in three different directions. The simplest volume we can measure is the volume of a box.

The volume of a box is its length times its height times its width. A cube is a very simple box shape. Its length, height, and width are all the same. So the volume of a cube is its length times its length times its length. If the length of the cube is measured in inches, the volume is measured in cubic inches.

This boy is measuring the height of a box. The volume of a box is its length times the height times its width.

cube

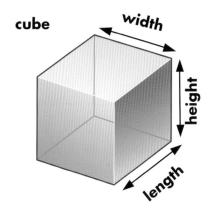

width

height

length

The volume of a cube, or box, is its length times its height times its width.

The volume of a square pyramid is ⅓ length x length x height.

square pyramid

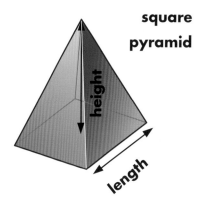

height

length

How big is your room?

Find a room in your house that is more or less box shaped. Use a ruler or tape measure to find the length and the width of the room, to the nearest number of feet. Ask an adult to help you measure the height.

To find the volume of the room, multiply the length by the height, and then multiply that number by the width. The number you get is the volume of the room. It will be measured in cubic feet.

By measuring a room in three different directions, you can find its volume.

Curved volumes

It is harder to find the volume of a curved object than a straight one. To work with curved objects, we have to use a special number called pi, which can also be written π. Pi always means the number 3.14. Sums called formulas use pi to figure out the volumes of curved shapes.

Volume formulas
You can use a formula to figure out the volume of a sphere if you know its radius. (The radius is the distance from the sphere's center to the outside). That formula is:

volume of sphere = 1.33 x pi x radius x radius x radius

The radius of this sphere is 1 inch. So, its volume is:

1.33 x pi x 1 x 1 x 1
  = 4 cubic inches
  (4.18 more accurately)

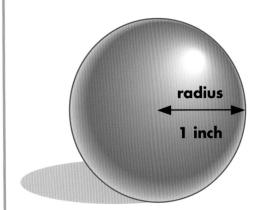

radius
1 inch

The radius of this cone is 1 inch. The cone is 2.5 inches tall. So, its volume is:

0.33 x pi x 1 x 1 x 2.5
  = 2½ cubic inches
  (2.59 more accurately)

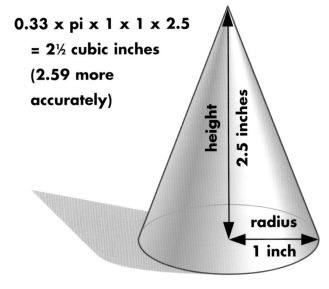

height
2.5 inches
radius
1 inch

There are also formulas for figuring out the volumes of more complicated shapes, such as a cone or cylinder:

volume of cone = 0.33 x pi x radius x radius x height of cone

volume of cylinder = pi x radius x radius x height of cylinder

Can you figure out the volume of this cylinder? Remember: pi x radius x radius x height = volume

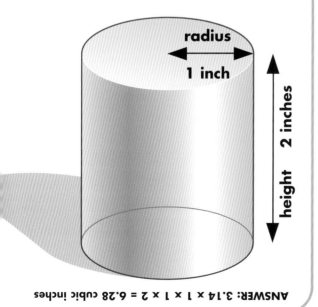

radius

1 inch

height   2 inches

ANSWER: 3.14 x 1 x 1 x 2 = 6.28 cubic inches

Engines, cylinders, and volumes

Why is one car more powerful than another? Car engines are driven by cylinders. Inside the cylinders, fuel burns, explodes, and makes power. The bigger the cylinders, the greater the volume, and the more power a car can make. A car with a 2-liter engine has cylinders that have a volume of 2 liters. That is twice as powerful as a car with a 1-liter engine.

Sports cars like this have powerful engines with many cylinders.

Harder volumes

Some objects have tricky shapes. So how do we find their volume? Many everyday objects are made up of simpler ones. For example, a dome is half of a sphere. Its volume is equal to the volume of a sphere divided by two. In another example, a pencil is a bit like a cone stuck to a cylinder.

We can always calculate the volume of an object by trying to find simpler objects inside it. We can figure out the volume of each of these simple objects. Then we can add together their volumes to find the volume of the whole object. So the volume of the whole object is the volume of the parts added together.

How big is the Capitol?

Suppose you wanted to find out the volume of the U.S. Capitol in Washington, D.C. If you look closely, you can see that the building is made up of a dome, sitting on a cylinder, which sits on several boxes. A dome is a sphere cut in half. So the volume of the Capitol is half the volume of a sphere, plus the volume of the cylinder, plus the volume of the boxes beneath the cylinder.

An aerial photograph of the U.S. Capitol in Washington, D.C. The building can be divided into a dome, a cylinder, and lots of differently sized boxes.

cube + square pyramid

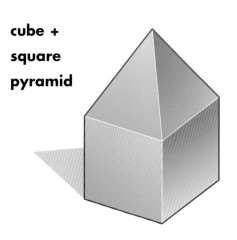

These more complicated objects can be broken down into a cube plus a square pyramid (left) and a cylinder plus a cone (right). Then it is easy to figure out the volume of each object.

cylinder + cone

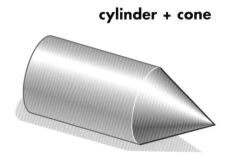

Estimating volumes

We cannot always measure things exactly. We cannot easily measure the volume of our planet, Earth. But we can still guess its volume. Suppose we could find a box big enough to hold Earth. If we could measure the volume of the box, that would tell us roughly how big Earth is. But Earth would fit inside the box with room to spare. So our measurement of volume is only really a good guess. We call a measurement like that an estimate.

If we could fit Earth inside a huge box, then the volume of the box would give us an estimate of the volume of Earth.

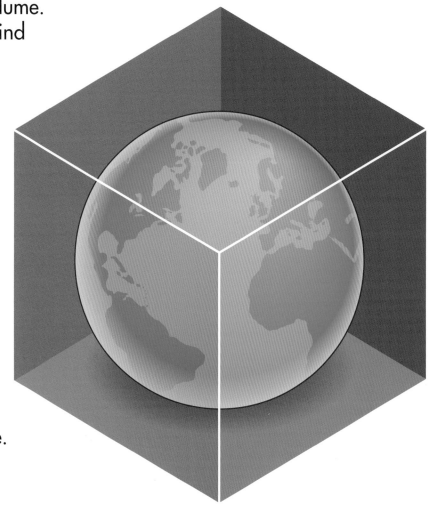

An estimate is sometimes the best measurement we can make. An example of an estimate is explaining the volume of an airplane by saying how many basketballs would fit inside.

The basketballs do not fill up the plane completely. There are spaces among the balls. So when we say a Jumbo Jet holds 30,000 basketballs, that is an estimate of the airplane's volume.

How much water?

The Pacific Ocean covers an area of 64 million square miles (166 million square kilometers). On average, it is 2.5 miles (4 kilometers) deep. We can estimate the volume of the Pacific by multiplying these two numbers. That gives a volume of 160 million cubic miles (664 million cubic kilometers). That is only an estimate because the ocean is not the same depth all over.

Pacific Ocean

Solids, liquids, and gases

Water is an amazing substance. Without water, no animals or plants could live on Earth. Like many other substances, water can take different forms—solid ice, liquid water, and a gas called steam.

The same amount of water takes up different volumes when it is ice, water, or steam. Unlike other liquids, when water is frozen into ice, it takes up more volume. When the ice warms up, it melts into cold water. That takes up less room. But hot water takes up more volume than cold water.

Steam spreads out to take up the most volume of all.

Making steam
When you watch an adult boil a kettle, you can see that a small amount of water can turn into huge clouds of steam. If we cool down steam, we can change it back into liquid water. That makes it take up a smaller volume. We can also make the volume of steam smaller by squeezing it. That is called putting water under pressure. We can do that by pushing together the steam particles in a special container.

Everything in the world is made up of tiny invisible particles called atoms. One or more atoms join to form molecules. The molecules in a solid are packed closely together.

The molecules in a liquid spread out to the shape of the container. The molecules in a gas spread out as far as they can. So a gas takes up the most volume.

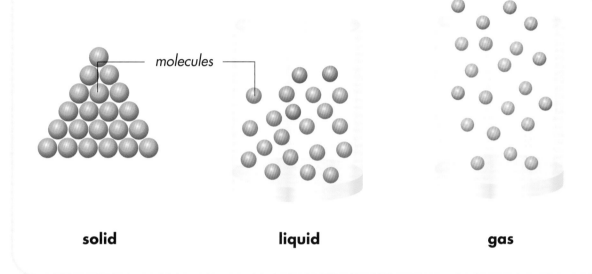

molecules

solid   **liquid**   **gas**

Amazing aerogel

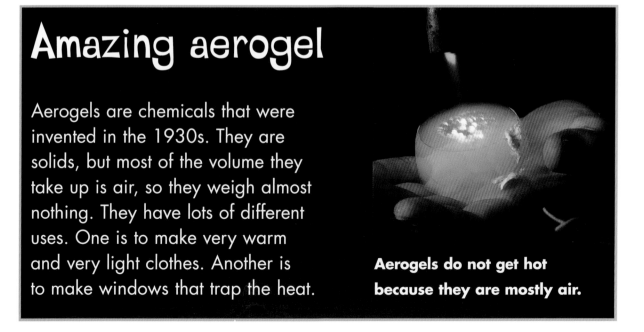

Aerogels are chemicals that were invented in the 1930s. They are solids, but most of the volume they take up is air, so they weigh almost nothing. They have lots of different uses. One is to make very warm and very light clothes. Another is to make windows that trap the heat.

Aerogels do not get hot because they are mostly air.

Changing volumes

We might think that volumes always stay the same, but that is not true. If you put a glass of cold water in the sun, heat makes the water molecules move around more. Each water molecule takes up more space. So hot water takes up more volume than cold water because it expands, or grows larger.

More heat, more volume

You can sometimes see power lines stretching lower in the summer than in the winter. Again, heat makes the metal wires expand and take up more volume. Even a huge building like the U.S. Capitol expands slightly in hot weather. So it takes up very slightly more volume in summer than in winter!

The volumes of things can also change during a chemical reaction. That is what happens when we mix chemicals together.

We make new chemicals that take up more volume than the ones we started with. That is the idea behind fireworks and explosives.

Power lines stretch and hang lower in the summer because the metal wires expand.

How explosions work

Substances such as gunpowder and dynamite are explosives—they cause explosions. When heated, explosives change from solids to gases. They expand very quickly and make a huge volume of gas. To start with, explosives take up very little volume. But the gas they make takes up much more space. As the gas is produced, it can make a violent explosion, which can blow out windows or even knock down buildings.

Fireworks are caused by chemical reactions. The reactions produce new chemicals with greater volumes.

Amazing volumes

Everything around Earth, including the stars and space, is called the universe. No one knows how big the universe is. It is constantly expanding. Its volume is always getting bigger. Volumes on Earth are much smaller, but they can still be pretty amazing.

Every day, on average, every person in the United States uses 69 gallons (314 liters) of water. That includes water for washing, drinking, cleaning cars, and making things in factories. It is still only a tiny amount of our planet's total volume of water. Earth contains a truly astonishing 330 million cubic miles (about 1,300 million cubic kilometers) of water!

Much of Earth's water is frozen as ice at the North and South poles. If all that ice melted, the volume of the oceans would increase enormously. The sea level might rise up to 200 feet (60 meters) over the whole Earth. Many of our towns and cities would be flooded!

The South Pole, like the North Pole, is covered with ice. If the ice melted, sea levels would rise all over Earth.

Big building

Space rockets are built in the gigantic Vehicle Assembly Building (VAB) at the Kennedy Space Center in Florida. The inside of this building has more volume than any other building in the world. It is tall enough to hold a complete space rocket on its mobile launch pad. The VAB is so big that it could hold nearly four Empire State Buildings!

VAB   space rocket

Flooded USA

1. If sea levels rose by about 17 feet (5 m), Miami and southern Florida would be flooded.

2. If sea levels rose by 170 feet (50 m), all of Florida and New Orleans would be underwater.

New Orleans

FLORIDA   Jacksonville

Miami

❶

New Orleans

Jacksonville

FLORIDA

Miami

❷

Equal volumes

Learn how shape and volume are related but different.

You will need:

• Some modeling clay
• Two rulers
• A pen and piece of paper

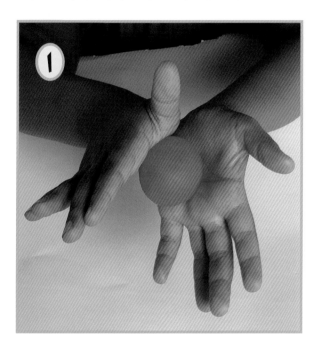

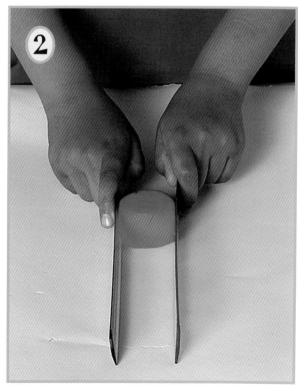

1 You need to make the modeling clay into a cube. A cube is as tall as it is wide and long. So, it is easier to make a cube if you first roll the clay into a ball. Make sure the ball is not oval (like a small football) but round (like a small tennis ball).

2 Squeeze the ball between the two rulers to make all the sides flat.

3 Measure the length, width, and height of your cube. These measurements should all be the same on a cube. Keep molding and measuring the clay until you have an exact cube.

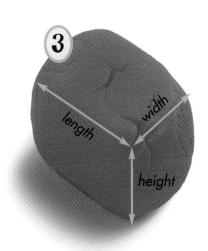

4 When you have an exact cube, measure the length, width, and height in inches. Write these measurements down. Then use this sum to figure out your cube's volume:

length x width x height = volume

Because you measured the cube in inches, the volume is in cubic inches. Write "cubic inches" after the answer.

5 Make your cube into a longer box shape. Squeeze it between the two rulers to make the sides flat. Do not add or take away any clay.

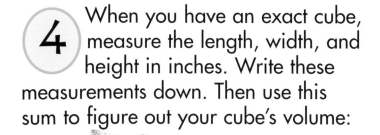

6 Repeat step 4 to calculate the volume of your new shape.

7 Compare the volumes of your two shapes. The two measurements should be the same. The cube and the box are different shapes but they have the same volume.

Glossary

area The amount of space that a surface takes up.

comparing A way of looking at two things together to see if they are the same or different.

cube A box-shaped object.

cubic foot A volume measuring one foot long, by one foot high, by one foot wide.

cubic inch A volume measuring one inch in each direction.

cubic meter A volume measuring one meter in each direction.

cubic mile A volume measuring one mile in each direction.

cubic unit A unit for measuring volumes.

dimension A direction in which we measure something. Lengths are measured in one dimension; areas in two dimensions; and volumes in three dimensions.

distance The length between two points.

estimate A rough measurement; sometimes just a good guess.

expand The way in which something gets bigger.

fluid ounce A small measurement of liquid volume.

formula A type of math we can use to work out a measurement.

gallon A measurement of volume. A gallon is equal to four quarts.

imperial Customary way of measuring things, which includes pints, quarts, and gallons.

liter A metric measurement of volume equal to a quarter of a gallon.

metric A way of measuring things based on the number 10. A liter is a metric measurement.

pi A special number used to work out areas and volumes with curves. Pi has the value 3.14 and is often written with the Greek symbol π.

pint A measurement of volume. A large glass holds a pint of liquid.

quart A measurement of volume. There are two pints in a quart.

reaction In chemistry, something that happens when two different substances are added together.

unit A measurement of something. Examples of volume units are cubic inches, pints, gallons, and liters.

Find out more

Books

Carol Vorderman, **How Math Works.** New York: Penguin, 1996.

Jean Kerr Stenmark, Virginia Thompson, and Ruth Cossey, **Family Math**. Berkeley, California: University of California, 1986.

Jerry Pallotta and Rob Bolster, **Hershey's Milk Chocolate Weights and Measures.** New York: Cartwheel Books/Scholastic, 2003.

Tom Robinson, **The Everything Kids' Science Experiments Book.** Avon, Massachusetts: Adams Media. 2001.

Web sites

Fact Monster
Information, games, and activities about measurement
www.factmonster.com/ipka/ A0876863.html

Math Cats
Lots of fun math games and activities
www.mathcats.com/contents.html

Science Made Simple
Metric conversions for volume measurements
www.sciencemadesimple.net/ EASYvolume.html

Yahooligans: Measurements and Units
Lots of useful websites about measurement
yahooligans.yahoo.com/Science_ and_Nature/Measurements_ and_Units

Index